# Day Trading for Beginners:

*How to Day Trade, Beginners Guide, Strategies and Mindset to Start and Become Financially Free*

Tony Toson

© Copyright 2018 by Tony Toson

All rights reserved.

The following Book is reproduced below with the goal of providing information that is as accurate and reliable as possible. Regardless, purchasing this Book can be seen as consent to the fact that both the publisher and the author of this book are in no way experts on the topics discussed within and that any recommendations or suggestions that are made herein are for entertainment purposes only. Professionals should be consulted as needed prior to undertaking any of the action endorsed herein.

This declaration is deemed fair and valid by both the American Bar Association and the Committee of Publishers Association and is legally binding throughout the United States.

Furthermore, the transmission, duplication, or reproduction of any of the following work including specific information will be considered an illegal act irrespective of if it is done electronically or in print. This extends to creating a secondary or tertiary copy of the work or a recorded copy and is only allowed with the express written consent from the Publisher. All additional rights reserved.

The information in the following pages is broadly considered a truthful and accurate account of facts and as such, any inattention, use, or misuse of the information in question by the reader will render any resulting actions solely under their purview. There are no scenarios in which the publisher or the original author of this work can be in any fashion deemed liable for any hardship or damages that may befall them after undertaking information described herein.

Additionally, the information in the following pages is intended only for informational purposes and should thus be thought of as universal. As befitting its nature, it is presented without assurance regarding its prolonged validity or interim quality. Trademarks that are mentioned are done without written consent and can in no way be considered an endorsement from the trademark holder.

# Table of Contents

Introduction .................................................................. 5

Chapter 1: What Does a New Investor Need to Know About Day Trading ............................................ 7

Chapter 2: What Is the Mentality of a Day Trader ...... 51

Chapter 3: What Should You Invest in to Be Profitable at Day Trading ........................................ 87

Chapter 4: What Are the Risks of Day Trading ........ 104

Chapter 5: Popular Strategies That Work for Day Trading .................................................................. 115

Conclusion .................................................................. 149

# Introduction

The following chapters will discuss all the steps that it takes to be a day trader. If you are ready to become a day trader and you have been preparing to get your series 7 licenses, then this book will be the guidebook to push you one step further to actually doing it. Day trading is a process by which a broker purchase stocks and sells them and purchase again all in one days' time. To be a day trader means that you are someone that has traded around 4 or more stocks within a 5-day period. This period must be contained in business days only and the trading activity has to have a value greater than 6% of the total activity for trading within the same 5-day business period.

Day trading is not something that should be taken lightly or on a whim. It will require you to be analytical, sound, and have a rehearsed strategy that will give you an edge for each trade that you made.

Check out some charts and ask yourself:

- How would you begin to purchase a trade?
- How would you sell a trade?
- How much are you willing to risk for a trade and what is the necessary size of the position would you need to take?
- What would the odds be for trades that are profitable? What tendencies would it show if you took the trade 100 times?

If you can answer these questions and still feel confident in becoming a day trader, then this book will help you get there. It is not an easy path to follow and it takes lots of time to get to where you are profiting enough to make it a day job, but it can be done and with copious amounts of research, training, and gumption you will be able to begin your exciting journey to the status of being an experienced day trader.

# Chapter 1:
# What Does a New Investor Need to Know About Day Trading

By defining what day trading is I can begin to explain to you how day trading will benefit your life and your Stock Market Trading strategy. Day trading simply refers to the process of buying or selling stocks in a quick way, for instance, you will buy one stock and then a brief time later when it has raised a few points you will sell that stock again, then when it drops down you will proceed to buy it again. This creates a pattern of buy, sell, and buy again. This process would happen on the same day. This also can be called a short sell.

When you perform a short sell, you will be required to do this in the margin account. However, if you sell short and then buy on the same day to cover, this is considered to be a day trade instead of a short sell. This rule applies to securities as well as options.

A pattern day trader is someone that has traded around 4 or more stocks within a 5-day period. This period must be contained in business days only and the trading activity has to have a value greater than 6% of the total activity for trading within the same 5-day business period. If the brokerage firm has any indication that you are a pattern day trader, they will designate you as one. This indication can be as simple as providing you day trader training prior to opening your broker account.

Once you have received a code as a pattern day trader, the firm that coded you will continue to believe that this is what you are, even if you refrain from trading for a 5-day business period. This is due to a reasonable doubt, based on prior activities. If you have changed your strategy, then you will need to contact the head of whatever firm you have housed your account with to change the code on your account.

Now that you understand a bit more about what day trading is and how it is determined that you are a day trader, you should learn about the requirements that a day trader needs for equity.

The minimum that is required for equity as a pattern day trader is $25,000 for every day that you trade. This is required to be available every single day. This must be placed into a deposit account before the day trading starts for each day and must be maintained daily. Your deposit account cannot drop below $25,000 per day.

In order to develop the credit arrangement for a pattern day trader, there are two involved parties that determine the margin account. This is the brokerage firm that is going to be processing all the trades and the investor. The brokerage firm becomes the lender that the investor will use to purchase the stocks. The investor becomes the customer or purchaser. In traditional trading, a $2,000 equity balance is required; however, if the investor is wanting to day trade, the brokerage firms found that they needed to have a cushion of $25,000 in equity for settling the accounts at the end of every day. This eliminates the risk of not having the money from the investor to cover any losses or fees. Many firms feel that the $25,000 minimum is quite adequate; however, they are free to ask for more equity if they feel it is necessary. You have the option to meet this minimum required equity amount with either cash or a blend of cash and eligible securities. You cannot use a cross-guarantee to cover the minimum requirement for the equity accounts of your day trading accounts. Each account must have this $25,000 equity line, independently. If you ever fall below the minimum equity line, you will be blocked from participating in day trading until you have provided a deposit of cash or approved securities to help you reach the balance that is needed of $25,000.

You are not allowed to trade stocks without supplying the minimum required equity deposit. If the brokerage firm provided this service of 100% loan to the investors, they would be putting the firm and the SEC into jeopardy of losing everything, based on the assumption that you would pay your debt in the event of a loss. The money must be deposited with the brokerage account simply because this is where the trading is taking place. The funds are needed for the required support that is needed when taking risks on the Stock Market. However, if you are concerned about anyone stealing your money, the Securities Investors Protection Corp or SIPC may provide you some protection up to the amount of $500,000 for every investor's securities account. The limitation is $250,000 per claim for any cash.

The buying power you have under the day trading rules states that you can trade 4x your maintenance in excess margin prior to the closing of the previous day. However, your firm will impose a higher amount for the minimum required equity and may even restrict the trading that is done to less than 4x your day trader's maintenance excess of margin. Contact your brokerage firm to gain all the necessary information that you will need to understand if it will impose these margin requirements that are stringent.

Margin calls happen when you have exceeded your day trade limits of buying power. The brokerage firm issues what they call day trading margin calls out to you. This gives you at most 5-weekdays to deposit funds into your account to meet this margin call for your day trading account. Prior to the margin call is met, the day trading can be restricted to a buying power of day trading that is only 2x maintenance excess margin and based on the daily trading commitment totals. If by the 5th day you have missed meeting the mark on the day trading requirement, then the restriction is further applied to trading only with cash that is available for a 90-day period or until the call has been met and lifted.

Cash accounts are prohibited for day trading. However, they can occur if the cash account is only trading to the extent that it does not violate the free-riding that is prohibited through the Federal Reserve Board's Regulation. This could mean something similar to failing to pay for your securities prior to selling them in a cash type account which will violate the prohibition placed by free-riding. If you do free-ride, the broker is now required to place a freeze on the account for 90 days.

This rule applies to every single day trade account. Many of the options contracts will require for you to pay in full for the options. Because of this, you have no margin options to purchase these options. You will also be subjected to intra-day risk when you engage in numerous transactions for options during your day trading day. You may see no profit on this transaction which you hoped for and you will incur a loss that is substantial due to patterns of day trading options. This rule is designed to have funds in the account where you are applying the risk and the trade.

Once the funds have been placed within the day trading, minimum equity requirement or your net any day trading margins must stay within the 2 business days that follow the close of the day when this deposit has been made.

## What Time of Day Is Best for Day Trading

There are many theories that arise during day trading, especially to the day trade and at what time is the best time to start trading. One of the best times to start trading is the first hour of the trading day. Recent studies have shown that the best times to trade are the first hour of the trading day and the last hour of the trading day. So, start simple and focus directly on the very first hour of the trading day. This will give you insight into what should happen throughout the rest of the day.

## Why Would the First Hour of Trading Be the Best Hour?

The very first hour of the trading day will provide you with some liquidity that is necessary to get in and out of the market quickly. The average times that the market trends all day are less than 20% of this time. Most of the new day traders will think that the market is an endless marketing machine which will move from high to low all day long. However, in the grand scheme of things the market is super boring. There is one time of the day when the market will deliver sharp moves that have volume this time consistently delivers in the morning. If this is what you do for a living, then you will need to have a seriously deep pocket full of money. This is not a job for someone with some simple lunch money. If you are proceeding to trade with $100,000/trade, then how much of a volume would you need for your stocks?

This is based on the price of the stock. You would need 10x1000 of shares to be traded every 5 minutes. You will need the volume in order to enter the trade. However, you will also need enough for a turn around to be a potential in a matter of only moments and close the trade that is just put on.

## What Exactly Do We Mean by the First Hour?

Here is a break down of what I mean by the first hour. In the first 5 minutes, you will see that the market has opened. This is the very first increment of time that the market is opened for. By most of the day, traders that have been interviewed the first 5 minutes charted can be the most popular frame of time. In the very first 5 minutes, you will see that there an insurmountable price and volume spike from the stocks that gap higher or lower from the day that is previously closed. This can often be the driving force of some earnings and announcements that are pre-market news. The very first five minutes to the day can be a very volatile period of the day that is chaotic at best.

There is not a range that is defined, as well as the odds that are present from the previous day will range and be eclipsed by the gap. When there is no boundary that is clear on where to go, the first 5 minutes whether a sell or buy can be a gamblers wet dream. If you want to take your career serious then you need to place no trades within those very first 5 minutes, at all.

In the example below, I will help you understand why this is especially important.

Take for instance this example of the NIHD, which can be a very volatile stock on the NASDAQ. This one stock gapped higher on the opening to a point of 9.05 and then closed lower at 8.73 later in the first 5 minutes. Next, over that hour the candlestick showed a lower drop. If you had placed a buy prior to the first 5 minutes of the candlestick and a short sell below the lower candlestick, then you would need to take it another step to place a stop order that lands neatly behind a higher/lower of the first candlesticks in order to box in the risks taken. It may seem simple but it's not. This is simply telling the brokers that you are willing to gamble with your money with this framework that is defined. This approach can be increased in likelihood for consistent execution; however, it is unpredictable and risky.

Next, you will see that some of the day traders will hold out for the first 30 minutes of the day. Often times the stock that is heading to fail is going to do that within the first hour, around 10 AM. So, this is your indication to jump into the market at the 9:50 time which allows you to have an entry into the 15-minutes that the trader has a second print of the candlestick and prior to the 30-minutes that the trader will have their first print of the candlestick.

Once the 9:30 mark and the 9:50 mark hits, you should want to identify what the higher values or lower values for that morning are. This will help you with identifying the lower and higher ranges that have presented that morning which will provide you a clear price point for the stock which exceeds the boundaries and can be used as the opportunity for going in the direction of the trend that is primary with which the breakout was traded. Or instead, you may want to go against the trend that is primary when boundaries have been set in order for them to reach and expectation of reversal that is sharp.

Once the NIHD set it's high or low for the specific range within the 20 minutes that are the first part of the day, you will have 2 options to choose from. The first one can be to buy the break for the 9:50 candlestick and head in any direction of the trend that is primary. Often times when stocks tend to b-line like this within the first 30 minutes, they will traditionally not continue in this fashion for the rest of the day. It is best for the stock to bounce from high to low before they decide which directional range they will take, and this helps them build momentum.

The second option would be to short this stock and have the expectation that NIHD will be reversed about the time that others start to jump into the business around 10 AM. This is not the best idea since you are only hoping for a reverse in this stock. There is actually no justified proof. By looking at this NIHD stock from this standpoint, you will want to stay with cash on this one. By sizing up your trades, you would have missed the movement that the stock created for the remainder of this hour. The next step is to enter the trade within the time period of 9:50 AM - 10:10 AM. This is based on the break or testing of the higher or lower points from the 20 minutes that started this market.

With this example, you can see a healthy fake but in order to see a cleaner example, you would need to look at Newmont Mining from May of 2013. If you take a look at this one you will see that the stock shot down and then build some steam while it moved even lower. This, in theory, was waiting for a breakout directly afterward of the inside bar or what they call the tight range. This will invariably lead to profits that are consistent. The thing to always stay focused on is that 9:50 AM to 10:10 AM is a window that allows for new trades to open. The trade is placed at 10:15 AM, and then you have traded within the first hour. This will only provide you a 15-minute window for closing positions. This does not apply if you are instead trading ticks. These are a sure way to ensure that your broker gets rich since you will have limited amounts of time to move the market in the desired direction.

Now, this is where we get to the last 20 minutes or so of the first hour. This is when you allow the stock to move in favor of you. It may not sound like tons of time put into this, but in the Stock Market, this time can represent a 40-minute sector of time since you first came into the trade around 9:50 AM. There are absolutely no rules that state that holding a stock longer than the 10:30 AM time is wrong; however, the key is to remove yourself from that thought that you need to let your profits begin to run. Holding your stock till 11 AM is just as fine as well before you let it unwind. When people tell new traders to unleash them prior to 10:30 AM, it is disturbing to me. With all the automated systems along with the investors that retail the clamor for pennies, it makes it impossible for the stock to move in such a way to be linear that allows you to sit and place your trades on autopilot. The copious quantities of head fakes can create more erratic behavior that is over the top and unjustified. A clear profit for your target is the most accurate way to ensure the money is taken out of the market on a consistent basis.

Within these last 20 minutes, you do not want to hang out to see how they grow. This is going to be a time for you to look out for what closing is looking like for your position and then adjust so that you have an idea of what you want in the position to close it. Having set percentages for the target that you may be shooting for while the other investors adjust for value bases for the volatility of their stock is the right way to go. However, over the long haul, this will not matter since you can adapt your strategy for trading with performance. The key is to ensure that you come from the position of pulling profits from the market out of wanting to, not need to.

## Why 11:00 AM Is a Tough Time for Investing

Now I will talk about how 11 AM is just a tough time for stock trading. If you have followed the Stock Market for any length of time, then you will know that the Stock Market is really busy in the early morning hours and then as the day progresses on it becomes less and less fluid. The greatest number of investors is taking part in the early morning stock market rise. Many people think they can make their profits in the Stock Market all day, however true this is, the problem is not that you can make money but that the majority of the investors are not making any profit all day long. After about 11 AM, the number of people investing and trading decreases. The reason for this is that those that are institutional investors or the ones that have hedge funds have an understanding that the work that is done during the middle of the day is a risk to their portfolios. This action that takes place during the middle of the day would actually be the results of sideways action.

Stocks tend to breakout with a rollover that is quick. Stocks have an uncanny way of moving in one single direction with volume that is normal for reasons that are not apparent. Price movements happen but they will be super small, and after the commissions are earned, the time fighting is spent, and the market becomes a headache that is worth it.

## Why Things Could Go Wrong in the First Part of the Stock Trading Day?

Although there is a consistent flow of money that can be made, there is also a chance of not making money. Below is a break-down of things that can go wrong when working your day trading during the first hour.

Things tend to get out of hand super-fast since first thing in the morning does not give you the opportunity to ignore stops. This means that if your stock drops from $12 to $6.15 by 9:45 AM, then this will show a negative percentage drop of 49% within 13 minutes. Consider this for a bit and imagine the impact this will have on your portfolio. Consider that you submitted a stop prior to the low of the pre-market range then you could have left with a 10% loss. This may still be a loss but it's not as big as the comparison of 50%.

This means that even if you are correct about your trades then you will still need to be fast. If you are trading in the morning with those that are fast, then you will need to trade using the information from a 1-minute to 3-minute chart. The action that happens within a morning trade takes place so fast that a 5-minute to 15-minute chart could be missing most the action that is taking place. Once the stock is moving in the right direction, you will need to take money from off the table.

Do not concern yourself with guessing the top or bottom. You will come to a period in your career as a trader where inevitably you will need to nail the top and the bottom. However, this just means that you are hunting a ghost. With the morning trade, you will find that it is more difficult to call the points at which the market is turning. The action is super-fast and that is why this takes place. So, consider focusing on the profit instead of what the risk is greater. This way you will need to have a larger sample in order to beat the market. However, you should definitely refrain from reviewing the older trades as well as focusing on who the winner is. This can create some greed symptoms inside you when it comes to trading. Take a more beneficial approach by tracking the losses and profits that you experience from each trade. This will help you to create an average sense of hope that will be based on the securities volatility that you have been trading.

Make sure that you are aware of the big losses

that can be triggered by the stops. If you have faced low float stocks during trading, then you should prepare yourself for all possibilities that could arise such as the 6% to 10% losses. The classic method that is used to assess this would be to place a stop below the candle breakout. However, this can present a mid to high percentage loss that is single digit at times. I am not trying to scare you into stepping away from the low float; however, you do need to be realistic when it comes to the terms of the money that is used on each low float trade of stock.

## What Are the Qualifications to Be a Day Trader

Day traders have several requirements that are needed to be met in order to qualify for this position. Having enough money is the only one of them. Because the day trader is actively selling and buying stock throughout the day, they are carrying nothing to the next day. All of these buys and sells are completed the day they are started. They continue this process of buy and sell all throughout the day and this makes their position a bit different from those who are just traditional brokers and investors. The day trader uses some leverage so that they can increase the industries exposure to trade.

So, what does it take to be a Day Trader?

They must conduct their business by starting with an honest self-assessment. To be a successful day trader, it requires for the trader to have a combination of not only skills, but knowledge, and traits that allow you to commit to this lifestyle. Are you capable of using mathematical analysis, behavioral psychology, financial knowledge, and the stomach for entrepreneurship? Contrary to the notion that is perceived for the easy life or I should say easy money, a day trader is something that actually requires:

- Longer hours for work.
- Exceedingly lesser amounts of work left.

- Continuous learning of self with no actual guidance.
- Abilities to actually take a risk with money.
- A commitment that is never ending for the activities that pertain to the job that is needed daily.

To be a day trader is that you need to have the right type of mindset. This is the first step to be a wonderful day trader. Start with a self-assessment that pertains to these points listed above. Unless you are prepared for self-learning, and devotion of time, along with a mental preparedness that will help you take risks and handle the losses that you suffer, then you should never try day trading. Consider checking out a few books on self-assessments to see if you fit the bill.

Make sure you have sufficient capital to generate profits on a consistent basis. Experiencing losses is part of day trading. In order to handle some of the risks that go along with being a day trader, you will need to have a cushion of sufficient money that is budgeted for trading. If you are entering the day trading world with a small amount of financial cushion, then you are setting yourself up to fail. Prior to quitting your day job to become a full-time day trader, you will need to have $100,000 to place in the account for margin requirements. A novice will be able to start with smaller amounts; however, this only depends on the plan of trading they have selected as well as the frequency with which the trading will take place. This can also include other costs for you to be burdened with.

As a day trader, you will also need to understand the Stock Market since day traders have to have solid foundations based in education, and knowledge about the functions of the market. You will need to have details that are simple such as exchange hours in trading, and holiday hours, all the way to details that are complex, which will include the impact of events in the news, requirements of margin, and a tradable instrument that is allowable. Traders need to understand that their knowledge base needs to be wider.

You will also need to understand that how to trade securities. This includes futures, options, mutual funds, stocks, and ETFs which make all trades effectively different. Not having an understanding that is clear about the characters of securities and the requirements for trading, initiating strategies that are involved with trading can lead to failures. A trader should know the requirements for margins for futures, as well as commodities and options that can impact significantly on the capital of trading. Understand how the interim of the assignment or an exercise for a position of an option and how it will shatter the trading of completely planned. Having a lack of the knowledge base about the specific necessities that are involved with securities can create losses. An up and coming trader should be able to ensure that they are familiar with the full knowledge of securities for the selected trade.

Be able to design a trading strategy that is suitable for selection. When a novice trader has entered the trading world, they can begin to select two established strategies to trade or more. Both can react as a backup for the other in the event of a failure or reduction of opportunities for trade. Once the trader has learned more strategies, they can begin to move on to a larger number of experiences which will build up their portfolio. The world of trading can be dynamic in an extreme way. Strategies with trading can be consistent with the money-making process over a longer period of time, but they can then begin to fail at any given time. The trader needs to maintain a close eye on how effective their strategy for trading is and how to adapt they are at using it. Then they need to make it custom for them, dump whatever does not work, and find an alternative or substitute that would depend upon new developments.

Integrating strategies for trading with a larger plan for trading is necessary for day traders.

Selecting the right strategy for trading stocks is not enough for you to be successful. You must consider the need for a strategy that is complementary to the plan of trading.

- Who will your strategy be used to such as the entry and exit strategies?
- How much money will you need to have?
- How much money do you need per trade?
- Which of these assets will you trade?
- How frequently do you plan to place trades?

As a day trader, you will need to understand how to manage money as well as how to practice safe habits of money management. Consider that you have at a budget of $100,000 of capital for trading. You have also developed a strategy that is excellent for trading. This strategy is offering a 70% rate of success. It means that 7 out of 10 trades have been successful. How much would you need to spend on your first trade if it's based on what you want to spend? If your first 3 trades become losses then this would affect your 7 out of 10 profitable ratios. How should you allocate the requirements that are money margins for future trades? With managing your money properly, you are able to address the challenges. The use of an effective management system for your money can begin to help you cultivate wins even if you only have 4 trades that are profitable out of the 10. So, take time to practice, then plan, and finally structure the threads that you do according to the management of your money and the allocation of your capital plan.

Consider the charges that the brokerage will be charging you. When day trading, you will see frequent transactions that will involve results of highly costly brokerage fees. Once you have done your research thoroughly, you will be able to plan the proper brokerage firm that you will go with through a carefully thought after plan. If you intend to only trade one or two per day, then you will need to find a broker that charges on a per trade basis plan. If you are planning to do day trading, then your volume is going to be high. In this instance, you should go with a staggered fee plan. The higher volumes that you have, the lower the cost will effectively be. You can also benefit from a plan that is a fixed rate. This will provide an unlimited amount of trades for one high fixed rate.

Apart from all of this, the broker also offers services that include utilities for trading, and platforms that you can utilize for trading. The integrated solution for trading can be things such as combinations options, software trading, data for historical accuracy, tools that help with research, alerts for the trades, applications that chart with indicators that are technical along with features that are not already listed. Some of these features can be cost-effective or free, while some may come with a cost that could eat a hole in your profits or wallet. You should pick the features that are handy for your trading needs and avoid the ones that are subscribed to help with specific needs. A novice can start with basic low-cost brokerage fees that match the trading needs that are initially set and then later they can opt for modules and upgrades that are needed at this time.

You will also need to be able to simulate or reverse test the historical data of the strategies and trading charts. Once you have set a plan and it is ready, then you need to be able to simulate it to test the strategy and utilize the test to run a virtual test account with virtual money. Many of the brokers that you can hire will allow you to run a test for your account. You can also use the historical data to backtest the strategy. This will give you an assessment that is realistic, as well as keep considerations for the cost of the brokerage and fees that subsequently will come up for the different various utilities.

## Do You Need a Large Amount of Money to Day Trade

What is the appropriate amount of money that is needed to be a proper day trader? The amount of money that you will need depends on the style of trading that you wish to do, and where to trade. This can also depend on the market that you trade in as well.

The US requirements for a stock trader who participates in day trading is that you have to maintain the balance on your account at an amount of $25,000 and up. If you plan to make 4-day trades per week, then you will need to start with $30,000. 4-day trades that happen within the same week labels you as a day trader, which makes you subject to the $25,000 account balance minimum. If you have an account that drops below $25,000 then you will be limited by the number of trades that you can do. The broker will place a stop on your account, so it is best to start your account with more than $25,000 in your stock account. This will provide you with the ability to have a buffer to fall back on. There are some options that can help you with day trading with less than $25,000, however, it is based on the country that you are in, or want to trade in. However, you still need to use a deposit of $10,000 into the account for your day trading. With a smaller account, you may need commissions as well as fees that will erase profits or erode them significantly. On a much larger account, you will see a cost of trading that is much less of an impact. One of the most common errors with new investors is that they under-capitalize their investment account. There are days that take place with losses. If you take a loss, then you need to be prepared to have enough money to maintain your account open.

You should risk no more than 1% of your capital. The risk is the difference between a price of entry and price of stop loss. Multiply this by the number of shares that you have purchased. An example of this is stock bought at $10 with a stop loss of $9.75, at 500 shares. The overall risk is $0.25x500=$125. You will need to have a balance of $12,500 in your margins account to cover the $125 since it is 1% of the balance. This is the minimum account size that is needed for this trade to be made without being over 1%. However, in the US you have to have $25,000 for day trading. This makes the investor able to invest up to $250/trade and still sit right in the margin of 1% for the guidelines on the risk.

## Day Trading on Forex with Capital Required

To open a forex account, the requirement for the stock regulations is not the same. Forex provides a leverage of 50:1, and higher within some of the other countries. If the leverage is increased, then the reward and risk are increased. Forex is the foreign exchange which is a market for buying currency from one country and selling currency from another. Currencies have a 24-hour trade schedule for 5 days per week. Because of this, the currency market is one of the largest stock trading markets in the world. The volume for each daily sale will amount to $5 trillion for bought and sold currencies. What makes it attractive for an alternative trading solution is in its liquid. An account can be opened for the Forex for as little as $100, however, starting with $500 is a much better option. This places you in a position to be able to place proper stop loss levels and place your day trades. With this small amount of money, you are not going to make a proper living from these trades. You can make a bit of money to help grow your account, but it will take some time.

If you want to make a large amount of income from your Forex Trading then you should start with a minimum of $1,000, but a better amount would be $3,000 or $5,000. This will allow for a monthly income to start building in your account.

# Day Trade Futures with These Capital Requirements

Futures are a popular option for those day traders that do not have a $25,000 budget to work with. The day trader does not need to invest the minimum that other day traders are required to invest for futures. The types of contracts are traded for all sorts of diverse types of products, such as natural gas, oil, gold, and some indexes. To be a futures day trader, the minimum that is required for trading is a deposit of $1,000. For an E-mini S&P 500 (ES), most of the brokers will require the investor to have a minimum of $400 to $500 for available capital within the account for a one contract trade. This is the margin for day trading. If you are trying to open an account with only $1,000 then it is not recommended. You should make an investment of $8,000 to open a futures account and more if you are trying to day trade with the ES futures. If you want to purchase other futures contracts, your broker will require some additional balance margins set. This means that you should start with a $10,000 budget which gives you flexibility with your available trades. If you use a strategy that is risk controlled then you will be able to build an income from that $8,000, even though you are only risking the 1%/trade.

### The Breakdown:

- The US requires $25,000 for a day trader in escrow.
- Forex can be started with only $1,000.
- Future Day Trading-contract like ES $8,000, multiple contracts $10,000.
- Test your strategies in a dummy account. Once you see a profit for a couple of months in subsequent rows then open a real account for day trading.
- Budget in a time period of 6-12 months.

### How Do You Get Started

Day trading is not something that should be taken lightly or on a whim. It will require you to be analytical, sound, and have a rehearsed strategy that will give you an edge for each trade that you made.

Check out some charts and ask yourself:

- How would you begin to purchase a trade?
- How would you sell a trade?
- How much are you willing to risk for a trade and what is the necessary size of the position would you need to take?
- What would the odds be for trades that are profitable? What tendencies would it show if you took the trade 100 times?

The only method for answering these questions would be to implement a method of repeating these strategies over and over again. You will then need to monitor the results to get an exact science. The strategy will create a tendency for a simplified way to find the action price daily of any of the assets, as well as a strategy which someone else can learn.

## Practice Makes Perfect or at Least Teaches You What Not to Do

Practice is the key factor for everyone who succeeds. When you need to be good at sports you should practice. Even for a job that is minimum wage the boss makes it a practice to do what is necessary before actually doing it. By practicing, you will have learned how to specifically protect your assets without losing real ones. By practicing using a demo account, you are able to learn how to trade stocks without losing a single dollar that is real. Take a methodical approach to the practice your trade strategy. You will find that there are not two trades that are exactly alike. Today's stocks can be volatile, yet tomorrow may be sedated, the next day could be booming with profit, but the next day can be just downright lousy. If you do not continue to practice then you may be faced with more losses than wins, until your strategy has been developed properly. You may find that you are missing signals about your trades and you may even become inclined to make a trade that is not part of the strategy. Only practice the strategies that you are working on at one time. Make sure it is perfectly perfected and then know it like the back of your hand. When you switch into live trading, you will have the added pressure of using the real capital for your trades so make sure you know your strategy. Practice until your demo account is showing a profit over a period of several months. Only after being profitable for several months you will need to think of opening an account that is on-live and uses capital that is real.

## To Start Day Trading, Know the Capital Requirements

Capital is what a day trader uses for investments. It is what a store owner would use for inventory. It is what a restaurant would use for their meals. In order to operate on full day trading capacity, you need it to operate, as well as how much you use for each investment. It can determine your income potential. There are requirements for capital that need to be considered for starting to day trade.

For a breakdown of capital, legally you will need to have an investment allowance of over $25,000 or more. In order to have a buffer, you will need to have at least $30,000.

There are a few accounts that have a minimum requirement; however, if you plan to make more money from your investments then you will need to have a sizable bit of capital.

## To Start Day Trading, Consider Goals and Constraints

Consider the constraints that can block you and find a strategy that will help you accomplish your goals.

- Do you really have enough capital in order to day trade properly? If you do not, then you should wait until you have enough to invest. While you are waiting, you can practice your strategies until you have built enough capital to go live.
- Do you have the patience to practice for several hours per day and commit to a

healthy or unhealthy practice of honing your skills?
- Once you have gone live with your trading, can you commit for 2 or 3 hours to trading in a stressful environment?
- Make sure you do not give up the day job prior to replacing your income with the day trading on a consistent basis. What times of the day are you able to completely commit to trading in the Stock Market? Is the strategy that you are using able to be completed in the allotted time that you have available to the day trade? Does your strategy fit into your lifestyle?
- Do you have the time to allocate a steady practice of practicing your trading strategy or building a portfolio, which can take 6 months to a year?
- Are you trying to day trade simply so that you can quit your job? Trading can quickly take over your life and could take a year or more to sustainably replace the income that you are currently earning.

Once you consider all of these questions you will be able to better understand if this will fit into your life and if it is something you really want to do.

## Choose a Broker That Understands How You Want to Day Trade

While taking the time to practice, you will be developing strategies that you can use for the rest of your day trading career. At this time, it is best to find a broker who will follow your example and help you day trade properly. This can be the broker that you are testing the demo account with or it can be a different broker. By choosing the broker that will handle your accounts, you are making the riskiest trade ever.

## Several Brokers That You Can Work with and Their Fee Structure

# NerdWallet

This broker offers tools that will help you with your financial needs. It also offers advice in order to help you understand options for you to make decisions that are best for you. Their guidance is objective, researched and independent.

## TD Ameritrade

- Fees per trade - $6.95
- Account minimum - $0
- Promotion - 500 commission-free trades and a limit of $600 with a deposit that qualifies.

## Ally

- Fees per trade - $4.95
- Account minimum - $0
- Promotion - $50 in cash bonuses with a deposit that qualifies.

## Trade Station

- Fees per trade - $5.00
- Account minimum - $500
- Promotion - None Available

## InteractiveBrokers

- Fees per share - $0.01
- Account minimum - $10,000
- Promotion - None Available

## Charles Schwab

- Fees per trade - $4.95
- Account minimum - $1,000
- Promotion - $100 bonuses in cash for a deposit that qualifies.

## EOption

- Fees per trade - $3.00
- Account minimum - $500
- Promotion - None, no promotion available at this time.

In the next chapter, I will discuss the mentality of a day trader and what type of psychology goes into being a day trader. I also talk about traits that day trader shave and how this affects their ability to prosper.

# Chapter 2:
# What Is the Mentality of a Day Trader

Day traders have specific character traits that make them prosperous and able to handle the stress that comes from dealing with the Stock Market and the fast-paced environment. It is not a secret that this job is hard and stressful, but what is a secret are the character traits that are needed by a broker so that they do not crack under pressure. 90% of the investors who trade on the Stock Market as a day trader will not make it. Winning traders have several character traits that help them be successful. Below, I will go over a few of these traits that can see you apart from those that have failed miserably.

### Rise Early and Shine

Waking up early is very crucial to your day trading abilities. You do not want to rush your routine for your pre-trading hours. When doing day trading, you are able to make quick decisions when faced with pressure and it is very crucial for you to be fully awake as well as an alert when the market opens. When you go on a walk an hour prior to working, this will increase your endorphins and give you a natural high that will carry you through the day with extra energy. This gets your blood moving and helps you get alert quickly.

## Prior to the Market Do Some Research

If you have stocks that have just been added to your watch list, then you will need to do the research prior to the market opening. To trade a stock, you should be fully informed about why it is moving. Being inadequately prepared can show up in how you trade for that day. You should trade with confidence and a little less uncertainty, especially if you prepare yourself completely prior to investing or trading the stocks. You need to know the key support levels as well as the intraday resistance that is listed on the charts daily.

## Ensures Trade Plans Are Following

Prepare a plan for all the scenarios that could arise with the stocks that are on your watchlist. They are well informed of where they will stop out, enter, and take profits all before they enter for the trade. Without a trading plan, you will be more stressed out and it will present as a more difficult accomplishment. You will need to prepare in advance.

## Investors Know That Trading Every Day Is Not Necessary

A winning trader can tell you that every day will not be positive, and some days are not good for trading opportunities. If you cannot recognize these days, then you will fail. When trading you can win or lose, knowing when to step back is necessary. To grow your account, it's just as much about avoiding the losses as well as the wins. Recognize the criteria that make it an A+ stock opportunity. This helps you to recognize when to sit on your hands.

## Reflecting on the Trades That You Have Purchased

If it does not get measured, then it does not get improved. Successful traders will track their trades religiously. Examine the wins and see what each one has that connects them. Then use that analysis to replicate this for future purchases. For those trades that are losses, you will need to analyze the common connections and avoid making those same mistakes. Eliminate the habits which lead you to the losing trade which is outside your plan of trading. Not every single losing trade is an actual bad trade. It is unavoidable for a losing trade to not happen so remember that it will happen; just make sure you are prepared for it. If you lose due to a rule of trading, then you will need to figure out why and then you can make changes to prevent it from continuing to happen.

Now that I have gone over ways that successful day traders stay successful, I will discuss other ways that show the mentality of a successful day trader and how to fix the mental game that is helping them increase their profitability.

## Small Losses Happen, Embrace Them

When working as a day trader, you will deal with losses. This is customary; however, you need to be able to handle it. Losses can impact your emotional stability and it can make a big dent in your confidence. You must recognize the triggers that lead to loss and can create a revenge trade, as well as some micro-managing which will influence us to make improper procedure changes or even dump a stock that we should hold on to. By embracing small losses, you will be able to fix the trigger of loss. A small loss simply means that you are testing the waters and doing something right. If the losses are sandwiched between some bigger wins, you will be able to handle them easier.

## Consider Your Next 100 Trades

Many traders can live or die by the actions of

their trades, or the need to make their next trade. Over long-term trade should be analyzed for the overall focus, and this should not be connected to the gains or losses of that time period, but the overall time period that you own the stock. Do not stress out of the one loss that you receive. In the grand picture of building your trading portfolio, one loss can be meaningless. Instead, consider obsessing about those 100 trades that come next. This can keep you focused on something that is not pertinent. The short-term is what you should be focusing on however you would be focusing on the process. When trading for probability, you will experience losses for good trades. If you experience a drawdown then you are not poorly trading your stocks. Do not let a positive trade with short terms that are poor impact the results of the psychology of the trade.

**Reduce Your Risks to Fight Back the Fear**

Placing trades can be scary. When you place your cash in the hands of another, you are stressed and worried. It is hard to trust that you will not lose it. Anyone that has been practicing trading who then goes out on there own must know how it feels to fear losing money. Fear can manifest into your trading strategy and keep you in a losing streak. It makes it harder to pull the trigger on a trade than it would be if you were not so fearful. Reduce your risk if fear is showing up for you when trying to trade. If your loss is small, then you will be less scared to trade. If your normal risk is $200 per trade, then you will need to have a lower $100 trade to feel less pressure and fear. Once you start to do this without fear you can increase your trade amount up to $200 again.

All these tips show how the mental psyche of a day trader works its best. You also need to put into context things that can negatively affect the day trader within his own mindset belief system. Below I have included several mindset beliefs that can affect how the day trader will negatively impact their trading accouterment.

1. Fear that they are missing some great move: As a day trader, they are conditioned to stalk the market for fear of missing some big break; however, they become more like a two-year-old who does not want to go to bed. They sit and sit, with fear that they will miss some amazing experience that will take place on the market. They fear that while they are away the market will continue to run without them and this creates anxiety about the loss of opportunity. Due to this fear, the day trader may find themselves jumping into a buy simply because he fears the loss. This can also happen for when the market free falls. This is an easy to notice point on the chart with the high or low within the print of the day.

2. **It is just not enough, even $250:** The day trader is churning out a profit of $250 a day from his $10,000 account. This is due to his steady strategy and system that

he has been implementing, although he is managing and trading for the good, he is not happy. He considers that $250 is not enough and that $500 would be much better for him. This is the point that greed becomes the deciding factor in his future profits. At this point, greed takes the wheel and starts to decide what to buy and when to sell. This creates a trigger in his brain that ripples into making all kinds of trading mistakes. He overtrades and stops sticking to his parameters. He experiences rampant emotions that resemble an angry football enthusiast, such as yelling at the screen. This is the culminating downfall of a lot of day traders. This is the time that a day trader will refuse a profit of $300 simply because it is not bigger and better. At this point, his winning trades start to turn into losing trades and his $10,000 account decreases to $5,000 in a matter of months.

3. The loving feeling that those who succeed experience and now create a need to continue that feeling: Take, for instance, the day trader has an amazing day on the market. Everything is going their way. They are having episodes of minimal stress elevation. This day is amazing in all ways. This overwhelming feeling of joy and warmth can create a feeling that is addictive. The day trader rarely feels this kind of emotional high, so they try to recreate it over and over again. They begin to add to their already existing positions. They double and triple the investment. This is similar to many who are super happy with his family. He enjoys their company and it brings him boundless joy. He decides that he needs to feel this more, so he heads out to find another family to add to his already existing joy. As we all know this can only end badly, so the resulting factor of over joyful and ecstatic for a day trader can create a need to feel

that over and over again and loses it all trying to reach that high.

So how can you use these negative triggers to your advantage? Below I have included a breakdown of how to use this to your advantage, whether it is you who are experiencing these emotions or someone else you trade with. When someone losses in a trade, the money from the trade simply goes to another trader's account. What this means is that these negative emotional mental blocks can become your payday.

### Using Your Excitement for Good

Instead of doubling or tripping down your investment, create a double stop to block these urges. This can be used in many ways. For instance, consider how much time you could spend in a private villa on a tropical island. Then place your trailing point stop 2 for 20 contracts. Then double the size of the position you are currently in. This means that as long as that trade is going higher you will stay, however, if the market turns I am removed from the position with a nice profit and I get short on contracts that total 10. This will use the market dynamics for emotions and take a clear and clean advantage. This sell-off will only occur from the trades of another day that succumbed to the emotional reactions for buying at the top because they feared losing out on the move altogether. It can also be contributed to the fear of missing the euphoria that you get in a win and when you have that winning position. After the market turns, the day traders that bought will be the fuel that needs to move down, and they will dump the position once the loss is too great.

## Consider What a Newbie Would Do and Then Snatch Them at the Low

Visualize what the newbie day trader would be doing at this exact position. For instance, you entered at a specific point, at what point is the pain point for a newbie? If the S&P movement was 6 points with no retracements that were meaningful then this would become UNCLE for the majority of day traders. Imagine that this is the pain point of the newbie and after this point, swoop in and buy up the stocks.

## Look for Those Ticks

Watch for those ticks that will come along. If the readings are over +1000 tick readings or -1000 tick readings below then you will need to fade out your moves. If there is a +1000 tick move and I have already gone then I start to exit the move with a short position. However, the reverse of this is also true for a stopping point of 4 ½ and a target point of 3. If neither is hit after 25 minutes, exit this trade at the price that is current.

## High Five Equals Sell

When I see traders going around the room giving others a high five for a good trade I take that as my cue to sell. This is a signal that I have noticed comes from extreme emotional euphoria and means that the market is in a good spot.

# Traits That Will Ensure You Succeed as a Day Trader

So how can you ensure that you will be successful at day trading? And what does it takes to be successful? There are 3 psychological quirks which will have an enormous impact on your day trading. As a day trader, we can face some troubling problems and most of these are going to be ones that we do not even know we have. Some of our human characteristics will affect how we trade and in the end our bottom line. Although there are several that can affect us, the five most important and detrimental are listed below with a breakdown of how they do affect us with our day trading. These can place a block in the way of us achieving the goals that we have set for our finances.

## There Are Several Enemies That We Do Not Even Recognize and Most of It Is Ourselves

When you deal in day trading there will be moments that we will err, and this can be fixed, but only if we analyze it and make attempts to adjust the err. If you have exited from a trade too early, you will find that by adjusting your criteria, you will be able to make a better decision. Make adjustments to this error by looking for an indicator that is different or takes a longer amount of time to make the trade. If your trading strategy is solid but you still find yourself losing some money, you will need to examine yourself and the psychology that we apply to the solution. When dealing with your own inner workings, your view is often skewed due to being so personally connected. You may not have the ability to fix the problem that is creating the loss. Your true problem could be created by a clouded mindset that is biased at best. There may be some trivialities that are superficial, and they are creating the discrepancies within your trading ability. For example, you have a trading strategy but never stick to it. So, this person is on a continuous adjustment period and nothing is working because it is not given the proper time to work nor the right amount of credit. By sticking with a strategy, you will be able to check your resolve for solving the equation. Your success record will increase by applying one specific approach that has a solid framework and foundation.

## There Is Power in Awareness

Being aware of the possibilities that could be creating the issues will help us to adjust them later. By creating actions which we can adjust over time, we can begin to see how each action is creating loss and change the habits that are contributing to this loss. We will overcome the problems that arise and be able to eliminate these problems. Since there is no magic plan that will make everyone a winner, this is where knowing who you are and adjust non-serving traits will come in handy. Psychology states that by being aware of our pitfalls, we can adjust them and improve upon who we are. This rings true for the day trader as well. Changing our habits and creating a profit will help us to be better at our day trading.

## Bias Sensory-Derived

By compiling information from the experiences around us we gain opinions, and this can create a bias with which will dictate how we operate. This will allow the investor to function as well as learn behaviors. However, as we understand that this is forming behaviors or opinions that would be factual in bases and evidence shows it is often not the case. For instance, a trader who watches the news and bases his knowledge on the reports will believe he has stripped the opinions from the broadcaster and is going on pure facts when he, in fact, is not. If our sources are all biased, then how can we expect our own thoughts and opinions to not be biased based.

There are always two sides to every story and biased is the basis with which these stories have differences. Constant exposure to a biased opinion can, in turn, make you believe that this biased opinion is your own truth even if it is not factual. Those raised to believe that dogs are scary will, no matter what, always believe that dogs are scary even if there are no bases for the truth. Since there is no counterevidence to dispute the bias, the opinion becomes their truth as it is the only available information that has heard, even if it is biased.

## Vagueness and Ambiguity Are Avoided

This can be known also as fear of the unknown. The avoidance of what is possible to occur, even if it has not. The avoidance of things that is not clear to our thoughts. This avoidance can prevent even a seasoned investor from doing things that would increase their profit line and keep them locked in that state of loss. Some traders have actually found that they fear the process of making money, and this rings true for many entrepreneurs as well. This is not a conscious fear; it is something that is deep within. The fear of the taxes that they will owe can be so daunting that they will fear themselves into losses. Expanding the zone with which they are comfortable can create blocks and worry that sends them into downward spirals of loss. This creates patterns of sabotage that is done by self. This can also create a bias about which industry they will trade in, making them fear trading in any other industry than the one they are most familiar with. The fact that this industry is declining will be irrelevant to them. They will simply continue to pump money into a dead horse. They avoid the chance of winning a profit by staying in familiar investments and associate this with uncertainty.

This can also be seen when the investor holds onto winners less time than they should and sells the loser way later than they should have. If the price fluctuates, they struggle to face the facts of the movement and then fail at determining the appropriate action. They also will fear the experience of loss and begin to make drastic and risky decisions that will place them in jeopardy of losing it all. When they deviate from the rational, they will then become irrational and start acting accordingly. This then causes the investor to miss the gains that potentially could make them increase their wealth.

## The Anticipation Is Tangible

Anticipation is immensely powerful and can create stress as well as worry and excitement. Since anticipation is connected to "I want" or "I need", the mentality is self-serving. Most the time our anticipations will take place way in the future and sometimes they will take place within a few weeks. Although these can be far in the future, they create an emotional enjoyment that becomes addicting. This addiction can become the focus of how we want to feel always, and this becomes the achievement instead of the reaction. This can limit our ability to see that the payout is now and block us from taking the payment with anticipation that there is a bigger one coming, and eventually we lose the money altogether or make ways less than we should have.

Easy money can find its way to our door. It is more than likely that it will be grabbed by the ones that think calm and collected about their trading values. We can begin to fall into an anticipatory feeling that becomes the consolation and not the reaction to the prize. Watching the changing of hands for billions of dollars can be exciting but if the confidence is not there, we can miss our opportunity to actually benefit from this changing of hands. This is like us subconsciously telling ourselves that we are better off dreaming and that this dream is better than the real thing. Wanting to become profitable has become the goal instead of actually being profitable.

By understanding what is affecting our trading we can begin to make changes for the better. The psychology of day trading can be an extensive research project in and of itself, but awareness of how we respond and what our actions are can bring us to better understand why we are at this point. One way to adjust our psychology is to remove the bias that is influencing our decisions. Use charts, since they do not lie. Remain objective and become focused on the strategies that will bring profit instead of the movement of price. Avoid others well-thought-out opinions and create some of your own. Gain knowledge of how the market moves and shakes. This will help you overcome the fear and the greed that will arise during a day trading career. Unknown territory can create mistakes so avoid the unknown by researching and gaining knowledge. Base all of our actions on an objectively sound decision that is made with knowledge instead of fear.

One of the Traders I have followed for a while stated this one day and I fully believe he is right.

*The psychology of day trading is:*

*Emotions - fear and greed - will have impacts that can be negative on your day trading accounts. By learning how we can overcome such emotions, we as investors can become much better at day trading.*

# 10 Principles That Will Increase Our Psychology and Reduce the Negative Mental Blockages

1. Be flexible and do not hold onto the attachment to a trade. If the trade is not right, cut it loose and move on to another one.
2. Changing how you view the market day to day is the key. What you think of the market today may be a completely different story tomorrow.
3. By focusing on what you are doing now you can make quick decisive decisions. Stop thinking you can will your goals to happen just to prove you are correct about something. Listen to the market and forget everything you thought was being told to you by the market.
4. Gain experience and you gain intuition. By observing and experiencing the market, you will be able to gain intuition that can help you make the right choices in the

market. Check the chars, the live trading streams, and maintain a log of the behavior within the market.

5. Use the strategy that is right for the idea. Start with a hypothesis and then build your strategy around that idea. Sometimes choosing the best trade is based on the underlying buy. You may find though that a currency or derivative is a better tactic to play. Seeking out the least risky trade is going to have the greatest potential for reward.

6. Draw a line that you will not cross. Before you purchase a trade find the point at which you can be proven inaccurate. Decide where your market needs to go and then examine what level you will base the idea on to invalidate the claim. This is the location to place the stop.

7. Consistency needs to be executed. Be mechanical as you can be, even if you are doing manual trades. What this means is when I see something that meets my

criteria then I will jump on it and purchase. When trading, you should not leave it up to the discrepancy of the investor's judgment. In order to win you have to tow the line and be confident in pulling triggers when necessary.

8. Embracing the risk and uncertainty of the stock market. You need to be able to see that a trade will be a loss prior to jumping into the trade position. Expect and accept the worse possible outcome. This will help with the focus along with the trade process.
9. Believing can be seen in the numbers. By following a direct and clear strategy you will see that the numbers will show proof of the effectiveness of the strategy.
10. Individual outcomes from trades should be ignored. Look at the collective of all the trades that you placed, not the 1 or 2 that just took place. Examine those last 20 trades and see where they won and were they lost. The outcome of an individual

trade can be masked and will dilute the bias that was encountered by the investor. It can block you from repeating trades from the past that were not beneficial. This will help with future decisions that will be influenced by the bias.

11. Use an equation to calculate the expectancy of your trades. The projected return is the expectancy of the period of time which can be longer than expressed. (Avg. $WxWin%)-(avg.$LxLoss%)-commission/trade

12. Mistakes happen, expect them. By making mistakes, you can improve upon your strategy. Accept that you need to leave the ego at the threshold since mistake happen and there is nothing you can do to block this. Each error is a way of learning how to modify the approach to obtain added information. If you make significant mistakes, then write that information down. This will remind you in the future and reinforce the lesson. Due to this, it

becomes an ingredient which provides an improvement that is continuous and essential to growth in trading.

13. Embrace the disagreement with boldness. The founder of Bridgewater, which is the largest hedge fund in the world, employs a belief system of independent thinking as well as a culture that is encouraging innovation. There must be disagreements that can be handled with thoughtfulness, as well as non-egotistical exploration to the mistakes that are made. It allows for weaknesses and strengths to create goals that are achievable. Consider the decisions that you would make if the people you disagree with had more open truths that would foster discourse. This will be a process for discovery to produce results.

14. Ideas should be collaborated on. Discuss these ideas with others to gain insight from a different point of view. When we talk to others, questions tend to arise that will help us know what is missing.

Thinking about all the factors can make a difference in the development of the strategy.

15. Seek opposing views out. If you can understand your opposition then you can handle knowing the person on the opposite side of the trade. This will give you insight into who they are. There is always room for advancement, no matter how much money you are earning. Instead of covering up the mistakes, you can begin to confront them and make things more successful.

16. Make your own path and follow it. What works for one person may not work for you. Follow your own path. As traders, going against the grain is best. If you follow others example, you can only go as far as they have or less. Surround your environment with the ones that you are most inspired by.

17. Consider the opposite and do that. Look from every angle and consider the

opposite actions that can happen. Prepare what will happen on the opposite side of the trade. Then examine how you can change the outcome. This gives you an expectation of what is to come in the market. Think of the person on the other side and what would happen if you were the other person. If everyone is purchasing gold, then this does not mean you should. Media and talking heads are not always on the right side of the trade.

18. Do so that you can learn. Experience is the only thing that cannot be substituted. Head out into the market and try something. If you do not find a solution that works, use it as a learning experience and move forward.

19. Block out negativity. The ones that surround you should only be positive about your life. This positive impact will change the energy around you and draw in a more positive response. Learn from the ones that are heading out the door, take

away their knowledge bit by bit and use it to make your life better.

20. Prepare and prepare again. There is no such thing as over-preparing. You can never prepare enough. But you still have to step your foot out the door and take that first leap of faith into the trading arena. A winner is not someone that works harder; they are the one that does it no matter how much they make, for the pure passion of it.

21. Luck shows favor to those who prepare their mind. No one can be perfect, but they can be prepared. You must have more knowledge than the other players within the market. To increase the luck that you will have with day trading, you need to prepare for the day in advance. The one who shows up prepared will have a much greater chance at success.

22. The mind of a chess player is an analytical one. Think 2 steps ahead and think about what the future holds. You cannot control what is taking place now, but you can

control how you handle the future. Focus on what you are least wanting to happen and then consider how you will handle it.

23. Learning never stops. When people settle within their lives they shut down the mechanism that tells them to learn more. This is not a great idea. This places you in complacent comfort zones that will not help you advance. In order to be profitable as a trader, you will need to continuously learn new strategy and study charts. Look for opportunities that will advance your strategy. Think about the market and how to advance your ideas and implement new ways to invest in your financial freedom. Life is all about learning.

24. If you believe in your abilities, then you will succeed. To be great you need to start within. This means that you must fully believe that you are successful.

25. Behavior is strongly influenced by attitude. To believe that you can build from nothing is the deciding factor in how you will

succeed. This will help you to achieve a greatness that others will not achieve.

26. Practice mental visualization. A visualization is a form of practicing being in the moment that you want to succeed at. This will help you see it and then achieve it. Visualize how you want to pay the stock market and then act in kind.

27. Seeing yourself as the ideal self. Prior to going to sleep, place a vision of who you want to be in your head and visualize the ideal self. Closing your eyes see yourself in this context.

    a. What does this ideal self-look like to you?
    b. What is in your general surroundings?
    c. What kind of clothes are you wearing?
    d. How are you making decisions about your life?
    e. What type of people is surrounding you?

    f. How are you approaching others?
    g. How are you carrying your body down the street?
28. Others are not you, their goals are not yours. There is no need to compare to what others are doing; you are your own person.
29. What advantage do you have over others? What makes you unique? If you were to sit among your peers, what would be different about you? If there are skills involved in any game, then at one point the person with the unique character will be the one that is a winner. In the stock market, the equity will move from many to few over time. In order to win at trades, you will need to act like the ones that gain all the advantage. This would be the minority.
30. Foundations should be solid and create routines. The foundation for success is discipline and dedication. To have a consistent routine then you must have habits that develop with the behaviors of

subconscious transformation. Routine is necessary for developing healthy habits for day trading. Day in and day out needs to be the same no matter what.

31. Focus only on what you are able to control. You have more control of the outcomes of trade than you think. You may not control the market, but you will control the actions that you take and the reactions that you have.

32. Meditation walks, and exercise is essential to self-care. Balance in life is important and the key to being healthy. Without balance, you cannot succeed. When in rhythm you will feel great, however, it can be damaging if done consistently over time. Take a walk and listen to a podcast to take some time away from your day. Sitting quietly will help you clear your mind. Meditating can rejuvenate your body and mind.

33. Be humble and question everything you do.

34. You are not invincible, you will die one day. Be careful because the market can be evil and will take what you have put your time and effort into.
35. Self-talk should be positive. This will have a strong impact on the actions that you take. This will reinforce a positive attitude.

Consider taking these actionable steps to improve the psychological mindset to become a better day trader.

Here are the actionable plans that you can use to become a better day trader.

1. Commitment is the deciding factor.
2. Be flexible when facing risk.
3. Execution is the key to every trade.
4. Expectancy is calculated and measured for accuracy.
5. Be accountable for mistakes that are made and then change them.
6. Only do what works for you, do not follow someone else's example. It could be wrong

for you.
7. Routine is a must. In order to succeed, you must follow routines.
8. An unfair advantage could make substantial changes in your profitability.
9. Be humble and know that not everyone is perfect.
10. Use visualization to make it happen.

In the next chapter, I will discuss what you need to know to be profitable as a day trader and what you need to invest in to make it work for you. I'll also discuss whether you can use the same stocks over and over again or if you should switch it up.

# Chapter 3:
# What Should You Invest in to Be Profitable at Day Trading

Day trading is never the same for each day. A trader that has been trading for a length of time that is longer than a year will find that there is never two single days that are the same. Even though there are no similarities to the day, there are still patterns to the trends. They will occur over time, but they will be hidden within a random movement of price that takes place daily.

There are five-day setups that can occur over a specific amount of days, and at least one to two will occur within one day's time frame. However, they will not all occur in the same days' time period. Learning these trade setups will help you to exploit the potential of profit.

## Context within the Patterns

Know the pattern and watching are not going to be enough for a successful day trading. These patterns will occur frequently; however, they only hold power when a specific context appears. Understand the action price in order to have a great entry in day trading. Identify when the traders are stuck, and the price will have cause to surge in a direction that is forced, meaning that the traders are selling. These setups will occur during emotional points. This is when traders will feel the pain or the greed. However, there is not going to be a definite that this will occur prior to big moves and it does not mean that there will be a result of big moves. We do not have an exact knowledge of what the traders think, or if the acts will take place based on these thoughts. By watching the action of the price patterns, you will see regular occurrences. These can produce results that are similar, which can improve the chance that the trade is profitable.

## Impulse Buys Create Pullback That Results in a Consolidated Breakout

Trading can begin in a move that is strongly pulled in one single direction. This will take place within 5-15 minutes once the market opens for trading. The Stock Market calls this impulse wave. The price of the stock then will pull back and then stall out. This forms the consolidation so that the price will move sideways for about 3 minutes. It must occur within an impulse wave range. The pullback or consolidation has to occur lower than the price of open. Due to the initial impulses direction, the investor will wait and experience the breakout that leaves the consolidation in the direction that is equal to the stock. Breakouts that head in the opposite direction are not traded. You want to consolidate and pull back if the price is rallied as soon as it opens. Next, you should wait for that price to be above the consolidated breakout price, and then the long trade is triggered. Consolidation must be, compared to others, small in relation to the impulse wave that is going to precede it. The pattern becomes less effective when the consolidation is compared to the large impulse wave. During the pullback, there should be a distinct pullback, as well as impulse waves that are distinct. If they are not distinct, then the effectiveness of the pattern is less and is avoided.

This pattern can be seen throughout the trading day and can be how a trend will form. This makes it a strategy that can be utilized on most frames of time and in the market. The most power-filled moves that a market will have will take place during the open of the day, which is why catching that first hour is important. It can mean important things for your portfolio and creates large impacts with your profitability. If it occurred later in the day, then it can create smaller moves in price.

### Consolidation Reversal Breakout

Impulses are not always followed by pullbacks that are small. There can be big moves that head in one direction. However, they can grow in the movement to an even bigger direction that is opposite of the original one. This is a reversal in directionality. Focus on the big moves that are most recent.

If the price dropped to $0.20 at the open, then rallies at $0.30, do not get distracted with that first drop since it will not matter anyhow. You will now have what is called an impulse for the upside. Watch for the decline in price, just a bit, and then consolidate the stock. If the consolidation breaks $0.01 then stay longer. On the reverse, you can wait for the pullback to go to the opposite for the impulse. Then you will see the impulse has a smaller pullback.

### Support/Resistance Reversal

This can be horizontal lines as well as diagonal lines. They will point you in a direction that the price has been reversed for at least 2 episodes prior. This will include that starting point. You should know that the support, as well as the resistance, is not a price exactly but an area. The setup is not required to take place near the support, nor the resistance. In other words, it can take place slightly below them or above them. This informs us to be on high alert, which is based on the fact that a reversal can be coming. Because of this, we will have to sit and wait for the consolidation that is near. There is a signal for trade if the break in price is above the support that is consolidation, or below consolidation that is resistant. If this signal occurs, the price of the trade that moved one cent higher than the consolidation close to the support and fall for resistance which occurs in the pattern. Leave the trade immediately if the resistance breaks above or below the support area. Consider that the trade of breakout could be applicable.

## Breakout Area Is Strong

This is a fashionable way to trade a breakout that is either above or below the support major area. This is, however, one of the toughest. Although the strategies above are preferred, it is beneficial to explore strategic options for special situations that can arise. Look out for a level that has pushed back the price for multiple strategies that are basic. This price will rally and then will reach 25.25 however, and then it falls. Although it performs this dance several times, it can struggle to break through. Once the area has tested that price three times more, there can be an assured day trades that are noticed. Suddenly the price is reaching 25.26. This can signal shifts of importance. Breakouts do not guarantee moves that are big. You may fail to produce a move that is big, and the price can break boundaries that are strategic and sparing. By making moves away from the area, you should see a significant move away from the visual that is price tested. The pattern can lose the effectiveness that will significantly become rejected by the price that is near the area. This means that you should see several rejections that have happened over multiple times.

Once the traders push the level of the price back,

it becomes a pattern of the power, despite the level that is sent. The price of the fact is opposite in direction for multiple occasions in the past. This shows that they have a greater resolve than the opposite directions the traders are going.

## How Do You Make Day Trading Your Job

If you have opened a broker account and begin to trade stocks, you are not required to have a license. If you plan to work for a firm to trade stocks, then you will need to acquire a series 7 license. This requires a specific number of hours in a classroom and then a test that will license you as a stockbroker. In order to sell and buy stocks for others, even as your own business, you will need the license. For your own personal financial gains, you can use an online brokerage account and earn money for yourself.

Series 7 Licensing is a test that is taken after you have completed a specific number of hours for training and learning. A job that involves trading stocks, bonds, and other securities and then you will need to follow the guidelines that are set up by the SEC. These regulations require you to have Financial Industry Regulatory Authority. This requirement states that you will need stock brokers and securities licensing representative. There are several options of FINRA registrations; however, the one that is most necessary will be the General Securities Registered Representative. This will require you to complete a class and pass the test that is called a series 7 exam. There are some limited exams that can provide you with limited securities capabilities. These allow you to trade specific bonds or options. Once you pass the proper test, you will complete the license requirements. This means that you can apply for your series 7 licenses.

In order to take the test and get licensed, you will need to have an employer sponsor you for the test. This means being sponsored by a FINRA member for the financial company service. You will need to be hired by a brokerage firm and then put through rigorous training and put you to work with a trading mentor. They will then sponsor you for the license as a securities trader. There are not that many pre-requisites that are required to be hired as a broker however, the licensing is required once you start to trade. Once you are hired you will have an agreement that states that you are employed only until and if you pass the series 7 test. The firm will oftentimes provide you with the training that is needed or the courses that will give you the ability to pass the test.

A self-employed trader is able to trade with no licensing requirements for trading within your own account with the broker. You have to use your own money and if you can not make it a successful career then you will lose your new career. If you begin with a smaller account and then use that to learn as you go, you will be able to profitably trade prior to turning this into your full-time work. Then you can trade the day job for a profession that is full-time and profitable.

Many of the day traders are trading stocks, although it is just as popular for a day trade to trade bonds, as well as currencies or even commodities. You generally need to look for securities that have these features:

- A trade volume that is large and highly liquid.
- Bonds that are volatile. You want changes that are frequent for the price because this allows the investor to make a quick profit.
- Stocks that are known by you. You need an understanding of what that particular stock's history in price is, and various events that designate how it will react to— economic shifts or earnings reports. This is a key deciding factor. Day traders will often only trade a selected few specific stocks, developing their expertise in the companies that they are trading. This will help them to narrow their focus so that they are not thinking too broad.
- Newsworthy stocks are a go to. News

reports on a stock have a way of triggering investors to buy or sell them. As a day trader, you will need to be educated about these events so that you can make trades that are beneficial to you.

This day trade is done in one day. Although you already owned 10 ABC shares, you decided to open a position that is new in some more ABC shares with another purchase that are initial.

- *Day Trade: (Buy 1 share of ABC, Sell 10 share of ABC)*
- *You start with 0 shares of ABC stock.*
- *Buy 1 share of ABC.*
- *Buy 2 shares of ABC.*
- *Buy 7 shares of ABC.*
- *Sell 1 share of ABC.*
- *Sell 5 share of ABC.*
- *Sell 4 share of ABC.*
- *Since there is one single change in only one direction within the buys and sells,*

*this becomes a one-day trade.*
- *Day Trade: (Buy 1 share of ABC, Buy 2 share of ABC, Buy 7 share of ABC, Sell 1 share of ABC)*
- *Two-day trades.*
- *Buy and Sell share of ABC 2x.*
- *You start out having 0 shares of stock in ABC.*
- *Buy 50 shares of ABC.*
- *Sell 15 share of ABC.*
- *Sell 35 share of ABC.*
- *Buy 10 shares of ABC.*
- *Sell 10 share of ABC.*
- *Since there are changes that are two x in the direction from buys to sell, this is now a trade for two-day.*
- *Day Trade 1: (Buy 50 share of ABC, Sell 15 share of ABC, Sell 35 share of ABC)*
- *Day Trade 2: (Buy 10 share of, Sell 10 share of ABC)*

1. Trading with the same stock every time is a strategy that will help you succeed.

Have one to three stocks that are you skilled in and knowledgeable. Become the expert in those stocks and stick with what you know. Trade only these stocks and use strategies to calibrate the plan. You will have zero homework or research to do since you will always be trading the stocks that you already know more about that is necessary for trading. This will give you the advantage or the next day's trading since you will know what you are trading.

2. Pick the stocks that have volume enough for you to freely change your size of position depending on the bases on the volatility side. If your stock is one day volatile, then take size positions that are smaller than the trade and with stop losses that are slightly larger than the other as well as targets for the trade. If it is quiet for

the stock, then you should increase your position so that you can compensate for the stop losses when they are smaller, and the targets are discussed later. This is a way for you to make an income that is decent regardless of how volatile it is within that particular day.

3. In day trading, the popular ETF happens to be S&P 500 SPDR (SPY). By day trading that ETF, or any other ETF/stock that you have chosen.

4. Run a screener for your stock every single week in order to find the two-four stocks which will provide a volume that is good and the exact volatility that you need, and then trade these stocks off and on all week. Do not trade any stocks that are not on your wish list or purchase any new stocks that you have not fully researched. This

can lead to losses due to uneducated guessing and poor strategy following. During the weekend, take some time to run your stocks or ETF screens again and again. This will help you find more stocks to add to your handful of stocks that you will be buying and selling throughout the week. You may notice that when you end up using the same stocks to trade week in and week out, for multiple weeks in a row, you are winning more each day, however having a strategy to switch up the ones you are buying will keep other day traders from catching onto your strategy and buying them out too early. If things are going super well, then you can stick with what you know and continue to trade the ones that you know and have done the research into. Many day traders are trading by sticking with what you have gained knowledge on and you are going to have success as a day trader. Over time you can develop strategies that work for not only these same stocks but others as well giving you an advantage over others who are only focusing on one set of stocks.

In the next chapter, I'll talk about the risks that you will face while practicing day trading and how you can avoid these risks.

# Chapter 4:
# What Are the Risks of Day Trading

There are many risks that come with day trading, and many of these involve losing money. However, a few of these can be more personalized. For instance, you could lose your confidence, you may turn into a greed monster, and you could even end up losing more money than you ever planned to lose. Below are a few of the risks that come with day trading and how this can affect your career, finances, and life.

- Severe financial losses can and will happen. The life of a day trader is stressful and can become even more so when you suffer severe losses, especially in the first month. Some of the new day traders never graduate from the losing status to profit status level. You should only be willing to lose the money that you are risking, because if you cannot afford to lose it then you should not be playing. Do not use the money that you need for your daily household needs because if you lose it then you will lose everything. Do not take out loans on your house or use your kid's college funds. This is the wrong route to go.

- Day traders are not investors. They will sit at the computer screen and then they will look at the stocks that are moving and examine the value they are gaining or losing. They would like to ride the momentum and leave the stock as soon as it changes course. The day trader does not wait to find out which way it is moving but instead, they hope for it to move the direction they wish it to. They do not own stocks from one day to the next since there is a higher risk that the prices will change overnight. This can lead to losses.
- Day trading is a job that can be stressful and expensive and requires full-time hours. They must continue to watch the market

throughout the day while sitting at their computer. It can demand a certain level of concentration as well as a strain in the body to watch dozens of quote tickers that fluctuate throughout the market with price changes at trend spots. Day traders can have expensive fees tacked onto their bills for each trade. The firm will charge copious quantities of commissions for the computers and training. A day trader should have an upfront price list for the cost of their trading. This will determine the cost of the expenses and how much they will need each day to meet the minimum $25,000 mark if they lose.

- A day trader will borrow money or heavily rely on stock buying on margin. To borrow money for trading is a customary procedure for a day trader. This can be a risky business. Day trading requires strategies that demand copious amounts of leverage for borrowed money for profit. This can be why day traders lose money and end up in copious amounts of debt. They have to understand how the margin will work and the length of time that is given for meeting a margin call. Day traders have a potential for the way it is over their heads.

- Claims that there is an easy profit to be had is all hype. Those advertising claims that preach about quick money are all hype. Prior to day trading, you should understand how many of their clients have lost their shirts, as well as how many of them have won big. If the firm you are working with does not have a record of these statistics, or they do not want to tell you, then consider going with a different firm. Think really hard about the risk that you will be taking; this can be over exaggerated when faced with ignorance.
- Keep an eye on the hot tips or the expert advice that comes from the website or newsletter of the firm. Some of these firms or websites will seek out profits from their investors by giving away a hot tip or help

with picking stocks for a small fee. However, if they are tooting about the easy profits of day trading, do not believe them. Check the sources that these tips are coming from and if they were paid for the recommendations.

- Educational training, seminars, classes, and books that are on day trading can be objective. Identify if a seminar speaker is going to profit from the day trading that you do. The teacher of a class can gain benefits by offering to sign you up with specific programs and an author may make a commission for suggesting another stock or option.
- Check with the state of regulator securities about the day trading firms. These firms must be registered with the SEC for the state that they are doing business in. Confirm that they are registered and check on their claims. This can be anything from problems with past clients or the SEC. You should also check on whether or not they have any run-ins for insider trading.

# Rules That Beginning Day Traders Need to Know

I am assuming that since you are reading this book that you are new to day trading and since that is the case I have attached some rules that you will need to follow in order to stay in line. There are 7 golden rules to day trading and below I have included a break down of those rules.

## Golden Rule #1 Have a Game Plan

Not having a game plan will be the end of your career. Do not hit enter until you have absolutely determined when to get out of the trade. You will need to quickly assess the game and employ stop losses and manage the risks to minimize losses.

## Golden Rule #2 Know the Timing

Knowing exactly when to start trading is key to a profitable day. The old saying that the early bird catches the worm does not work with this situation. If you have read this far then you will know that in the first chapter I talked about the best time to trade and the first 15 minutes of the day was not it. The most active time of the day is the time when people make trades out of panic. There are also a lot of orders from the night before market. Keep your eyes open for a reversal. Many long-time traders will avoid the 15 minutes that start the day.

## Golden Rule #3 Margins Should Be Avoided or at the Least Cautious

Being swayed by a margin is something that will happen with all new investors. However, this is a loan and it does need to be paid back. If you lose the money, you are in debt for a majorly large-sum. It can increase your investment margin and it can also decrease your profit in the long run when you have to return the money with interest. This interest can be similar to a credit card. Learn to trade profitably prior to using the margin you are heading toward that route.

## Golden Rule #4 Practice with Some Demo Accounts

A demo account can help you gain some practical insights into how the day trading business works. You will have nothing to lose but everything to gain. The demo accounts can be done with a money account that is simulated so that you can gain knowledge of how to manage your accounts. This gives you the room to fail and to win until you have a perfect strategy. Many of the brokers that you can sign up with will have a free parking demo account that can be used to grasp charts, strategies, patterns, and how to handle the first 15-minute trading time rule.

## Golden Rule #5 Be Able to Accept That You Will and Have Lost

Learning to lose is something that all traders have learned to accept and come to terms with. Even the successful traders are well aware that they will fail at sometimes. To lose does not make you a loser but it does give you an opportunity to learn. Limit your losses and learn how to do that.

This is an important way to manage your accounts.

## Golden Rule #6 Absorb All the Materials and Knowledge That You Can

Having natural skills will help you in the long run, but you will need to learn how to train yourself to use those skills successfully. The most successful traders will not become complacent in learning. They search for the edge that they have and learn how to use it properly. Use a large number of resources to build the knowledge that is needed to become a successful trader. There are tools such as books, videos, training classes, and blogs that can be used to learn all you can. Since the market is ever changing, you need to be ever changing as well.

## Golden Rule #7 Tips Should Be Evaluated

We often receive helpful advice from friends and family all the time, but receiving unverified tips from a broker friend can be disastrous to your financial plan. It can even be cause for criminal charges. If you lose money, then you could have lost a lot of money from taking the advice that was not research. If you gain and money that is later found to be insider trading, it can land you in jail. Using your own experiences will help you to make proper choices instead of missing the mark altogether due to following someone else's tip. Check all the trading tips you get thoroughly prior to making purchases.

As with anything in life, there are taxes that can be assessed for any and all fees that are won during trading or income earned. Below I will discuss the taxes that you can be assessed for your day trading.

The tax rules on income can vary greatly. There is no PDF on how much you will need to pay in taxes on the money that you acquire from day trading, but I can give you a bit of insight into how it works. Tax rules vary based on your location and the amount of money you have earned along with what you are trading. These are all factors that come into play when it comes to taxes on day trading income. Although you are able to trade in multiple regional markets online, you will still need to pay taxes based on each locality. Tax rules apply in every region. You can live in India, Australia, and anywhere else, still you are going to be taxed. Each country has its own tax brackets to go by. The consequences that will be imposed on you can be extreme and costly. The day trading rules that have been set with the IRS will be different from those that are set by the HMRC. Make sure you follow the rules and find out the amount and type of tax you are liable for. Is it personal taxes, business taxes, or taxes for capital gains? You should also find out if you will pay domestic taxes as well as abroad.

In the next chapter, I will talk about strategies that will take you from novice to expert in the day trading market.

# Chapter 5:
# Popular Strategies That Work for Day Trading

Strategies are especially important to win at day trading. You will need to develop strategies that can be utilized over and over again so that you can continuously build a profitable portfolio. Below I have included several diverse ways to incorporate strategies into your day trading program.

Having momentum is day trading's all about. The first thing I learned when I started to trade stocks is I learned that locating stocks that are moving in price will be how you can begin to profit. In every single day, there are stocks that will move in price by 20-30% and sometimes, even more, depending on the day. So how do you identify the stocks that are fixing to make moves that could be big? One of the biggest realizations that come from day trading is that those stocks that move

20-30% the shares will have limited technical indicators.

In order to have a momentum stock trading strategy, you will need stocks that are moving. If the stock is sideways or chopping, then it will be useless. Locating the stocks that are fixing to make a huge move is the first step. Using stock scanners to locate these is the first thing that you can do.

Momentum stocks will have a few things that are similar. By scanning 5,000 stocks you can ask for the criteria that are true to what you need. There should be a listing of at least 10 stocks per day. These will contain the ones that have 20-30% move. These stocks will help you make a living as a day trader.

Criteria #1 - under 100mil shares that float.
Criteria #2 - charts daily that are strong.
Criteria #3 - at least 2x the volume for a volume that is high.
Criteria #4 - catalysts that are fundamental such

as PR, FDA announcements, Earnings, Investor activist as well as other kinds of news that is breaking. These stocks may also experience some momentum with a catalyst fundamental. If this happens then it is going to be called a breakout technical.

Using scanners to locate my stocks for day trading is an effective way to find the ones with the criteria you need. The scanners are more valuable as a tool that many of the new traders understand. Once the scanners pick up something, it will get alerted to that stock. Then you will have to review the candlestick chart in order to gain entry on the back pull first. Most investors will find that they need to buy this spot as well. These buyers then subsequently create spikes with the volume and subsequent results that are priced for quick sales as well as helping the stock move up. You should learn as a new trader to find an entry that shows in real time. Scanners are able to give advice for copious amounts of trade alerts on a daily basis. Instead of flipping continuously through charts, I am able to see the charts I need in a quicker more relatable way. Every trader needs to be using the scanners to find hot stocks that will help them profit daily.

Blue flags are a wonderful way to chart patterns. This is a pattern that is seen every single day during the day trading hours. It can offer a risk of entry that is low in a stock that is strong. The hardest thing is that the traders have difficulty locating these patterns in the real-time. You can locate these stocks by scanning them in the scanners. If I use the surging up scanner, I can find the highest volume relative to the market. By reviewing the scanners, I can alert to the strong stocks that I will identify at a given time of day. Pattern-based traders will look for all the patterns in the stocks that will support the momentum that is continued over time. Scanners will not be able to chart the patterns that they find. This is what you will need to help with. Maintain skills to justify each trade.

## Bull Flags #1 Strategy

With this strategy, the first candle would be to make the high anew once the breakout happens. Now scan for the stocks and begin to squeeze up so that the green candles in the chart of the bull flag. Then the investor will wait for 2-3 candles that are red to pullback with a form. The very first candle that is green needs to make a new high once the pullback entry is at the stop that is low. This will typically show a spike in volume in the moment of the first candle that is making a high. This means that 10s of 1000s of traders are positioning themselves to take and send an order for a buy.

## Flat Top Breakout #2 Strategy

This is similar to the bull flag strategy; the only difference is the pullback which is a flat top that has a resistant strong level. This will happen over a period so candles that are easy to recognize within the chart by the pattern that is obviously a flat top. This is a pattern that will form due to a big seller that has a specific level of price that can require the investors to purchase all available shares prior to the prices going higher for a continuing time. This pattern can have breakouts that are explosive for the seller's short notice which is resistant forming levels which will place a stop order right above them. If the buyer takes out the level of resistance, it can be a stop order buy which will trigger the stock to shoot a very quick high and the longs can be a nice profit if it does.

## Momentum Stocks and Where to Set My Stops

I tend to set a stop order that is tight when I buy momentum stocks. This stop order is placed just below the back pull that is the first. If this stop is farther away than the 20 cents away, then you may need to place the stop order less than 20 cents and return later for a second try. The reason for the stop at 20 cents is for the 2:1 ratio of profit loss. Lastly, I risk 20 cents due to the potential to make double. When you risk 50 or more you will need to make 1.00 to get a ratio of profit loss properly. This will make the trade justified. Try to avoid trades which would generate profits that are large for a trade that is justified. You will have a better chance of achieving a more successful trade for a stop of 20 cents and target at 40 cents vs the 11.00 stop and the target of 2.00 profits.

Try to balance the risk across any and all trades made. When calculating risk, you will see an entry price at your stop for a look at the distance. If your stop is 20 cent and you want to max the risk, keep it at $500 and take it to 2500 shares (2500x.20=500)

## Time of Day This Works Best

This is best used at the hours of 9:30-4 PM. The morning, as we addressed in the first chapter, is one of the best times to trade. So, as we discussed focus on the 9:30-11:30 time period, this does not mean that any time during the day we are not able to get a news spike that should suddenly bring about amounts of volume that is tremendous in stock. This stock will have shown no interest early and then becomes a great candidate for the pullback first. This pullback that is first will be a bull flag. Once 11:30 AM arrives then the only trade-off that is done is the 5-minute chart. This is because the 1-minute chart has become choppy in what are midday as well as a trading hour through to the afternoon.

## Checklist for Entry

*Criteria entry #1*
Momentum trading chart day pattern

*Criteria Entry #2*
The tight stop will support the 2:1 ratio of profit loss.

*Criteria Entry #3*
Volume is high, 2x or more, and associated with the catalyst. The volume getting heavier means that people tend to watch it.

*Criteria Entry #4*
Under 100mil shares, the float is low, however, under the 20mil share that is ideal.

## Indicators for Exits

*Indicator exits #1*
Sell ½ when the target profit first hits. I risk $100 with hopes to make $200. Once the $200 is up, I sell ½. Then I adjust the stop for my price entry with the position of balance.

*Indicators Exit #2*
At the point that I have not sold ½, the candle that is first to close red is the indicator for the exit. If ½ is sold, I'll hold the candle that is red until my stop breakeven has not hit.

*Indicator exit #3*
The bar for extension will force me to lock at the beginning of my profits prior to the reversal inevitably begins. Bar extension is a candle which spikes up and then instantly places me up by $2-400 or more. When I have a spike in the stock, I get lucky and sell into it.

## Analyze These Results

A successful trader will have metrics that are positive for their trades. Trading in stock is a statistical career. You will either have a return/loss that generates the statistics. When working with investors, the ratio for profit and loss and their success percentage is reviewed on a regular basis. By these statistics, they will be able to see if the commitment is there or profitability has potential. This can be done without looking into their P/L total. After you have finished every week you will need to analyze results that help you with your current metrics for trading, to understand the strategies needed.

The investors that are keeping a meticulous record for trades are the best because they are data mining the records that help you understand how they can improve their trading. Using a monitoring system, you are able to follow your stats for trading and this can be a huge help when tuning your strategies into a fine plan.

There are several strategies for trading that can be used similarly to the one listed above. Below is a breakdown of each one of the trading strategies that I have found will work for day trading.

## Momentum Trading

The investor jumps on the stock that has a moving price that is going up. Look for these things to use this strategy:

- Prices that move in a unique and major way. Driven by earnings growth and surprise catalysts. The new launch for a drug company. Buyouts of smaller companies by larger ones.
- Movement of 30-40% in the stocks.
- A reduced number of shares that are outstanding can be traded faster by smaller stocks.
- Tools like StockTwits used for trading to maintain the momentum through ideas and trends with a platform for communications that are financial.

Protect your assets from oversized losses. Warrior trading will set an order for a stop loss right under the first decline price. This loss stop will work as a form of insurance. Place an order sell for a predetermined price for the stock, that way the quote drops from a specific point, then the shares are sold automatically to protect the loss from further happening.

## Strategy for Scalping

Small wins equal copious amounts of money. This is the philosophy behind this strategy. In this process, the scalper assigns a target for the buy or sells. They then stick to the level that is predetermined. This strategy can be fast, so the traders will make these trades within a few seconds.

This is a better option for day traders that have been trading for a long time. They can make decisions that are quick and can be acted on without any question or remorse. Those who use the scalping strategy have the potential to discipline themselves to immediately sell the price decline for the witness. This will help to reduce the amount of loss. If you have trouble with a focus that is razor sharp, then this is not the strategy for your trading.

## Strategy for Pullback Trading

In this strategy, the pullback is the first step to look for the ETF or stock within the trend that is established. Monitor the price decline to show the trend. If this trend is established in an upward fashion, then the movement for price downward or pullback is a point of entry for the buy of the day trader. They understand the charts that are technical to understand the trend of the stock. Fidelity tells us of two successive movements for the high price of the uptrend prior to the pullback of the decline in price. Had we shorted the stock the two decreases in a row of price would present? If this reverses the trend, then the need to panic continues to be trending directional for a long while. The biggest gains will be seen with the pullback from the candidates from the stocks.

## Trading Breakout

When the price is top resistance and rise above the stock price, then the breakout takes place. You need to monitor stock trading levels for volume and shares which breakout trades have hands changing on a volume of high and are more sustainable and likely to have a price that is higher than before, and this can create a volume that is less of a breakout from what Fidelity says. It becomes more difficult to profit if the decline is with the levels of resistance and is more accessible to breakouts of lower volumes. The stock begins to retreat once the resistance level is being hit and there is a stronger movement of price with a catalyst. Beyond the price that is specific, the investors are preventing the rise of the price.

## Trading News

Stocks will quickly react to an event in the news so if you miss some numbers for earnings then this can cause prices in stock to fall. The FDA decides to approve a drug that is new can cause this to take off in the stock market. If you keep the news that is about business in your mind, then the day traders will show daily stories that they can capitalize on. If the news that comes out is bad, then you will be able short the trade during your day trading and begin to borrow the shares from stocks that are in the firm and those shares are then the borrowed shares are sold. When the stock declines in the price, you can buy it back at a lower price. The difference is the profit for the payment of fewer commissions. When the news is positive, the shares rise, and the price of the stock tells you to go long or simply buy outright.

Strategies are objective in nature. They can be specific to the individual as well as to the particular style of trading. There are several ways to build a strategy that will help you responsibly buy stocks and prosper with determined intent. Below are yet a few more basic tips that can help you when building your day trading portfolio.

# 10 Basic Day Trading Tips

## Knowledge Is Your Best Power

Keep informed on the newest news about the stock market, as well as events that can cause changes in stock. Interest rates and economic outlook is designed by FED's plan. Do some fundamental research and make a stock wish list of those that you would love to trade as well as keeping informed about yourself and the companies that you selected, and the market generalities. Scan your newspaper for the business section and then the websites for financial reliability.

## Determine the Amount to Set Aside

How much money are you willing to set aside for trade? Most of the day traders are successful and they risk less than the 1-2% for the trade per account. Your account is $40,000, this means you are willing to risk the 0.5% of the capital gained for a trade. The loss per trades maximum cost is $200 (0.005x$40,000). Set the surplus of funds aside for trade and when you lose you are prepared.

## When Are You Setting It Aside

Day trading is not a fly by night decision. It requires you to figure out the amount of time during the day for most of the day. Consider the spare hours that you have which are limited. The process of day trading will be to track the market and locate opportunities in your time that allow for you to trade during the optimal hours. Fastly moving is key.

## Small Starts Are Key

It is advisable for the focus to be the maximum of the two stocks prior to a session of trading that day. Tracking opportunities and finding them is easier with a few small stocks.

## Penny Stocks Should Be Avoided

Deals and low prices are great but staying clear of penny stocks is the best option. These stocks are not liquid and your opportunity to hit a payout that is great can be bleak.

## Trades Should Be Timed

The market opens, and the investors place their orders and the trades begin to work in their favor and they contribute to the volatility of price. Seasoned investors will see the patterns and then make the profits from appropriate picks. It is far better to study the market and hold all moves for the 15-20 minutes that take place at the beginning of the day. The hours in the middle can be useless and volatile. However, movement picks up right before the closing bell goes off for the day. It is safer for new investors to avoid the rush hours which offer tons of opportunities for growth in the market.

## Use Limit Orders to Cut Losses

Will you be using a limit order or a market order? If you place a market order, you should execute it at the price that is best for the available time being and gives no guarantee of price. A limit order will guarantee that the price is executed. Limit orders get treated with more precision. The price you have set is executed for selling and buying

## Profits Need to Be Based on Realism

To be profitable, the strategy does not have to be a winner every time. Many investors win only about 50-60% of the trades they make. They make much more money on those they win than the ones that they lose from the loss. Specific percentages of the account are limited to make sure of risks with each trade and this entry or exit method can clearly be defined by writing in your tracking charts.

## Remain Calm during Trades

There are moments when you test your nerves while playing the stock market. As the day trader, you will have to learn for you to keep greed, fear, and hope in check. Decisions should not be emotion based however they should be logically based.

## Make Plans and Stick with Them

Successful investors have to think on their feet and be fast about decisions, but they do not have to be fast thinkers. Why? This is because as a successful trader, they have designed a strategy for trading in advance. They also have a discipline that makes them stick to that specific strategy. You should follow the formula that you set up closely instead of chasing profits.

## Decide What You Are Buying and When You Will Be Buying It

Day traders are intent on making as much money they can by exploiting the price every minute there is movement in each individual asset. By leveraging capital in copious amounts, you can do this. A day trader typical looks for three things:

- Liquidity allows the investor to buy or sell a stock at a price that is good
- Volatility can be a simple measure that gives the investor the price that is expected daily with that specific range. This range is one in which the day trader will operate. Greater profit or loss means that there will be more volatility.
- Trading volume measures the

number of times a stock is traded in any amount of time which is considered within a trading day. A higher volume degree indicates that the interest has risen in the stock. Oftentimes, increases of volume in any given stock can be a harbinger of a jump in the price, whether it goes up or down.

Once there is a clearly defined idea of what stocks you will be trading, you must learn to identify the points of entry. Point of entry is the precise period in time that you need to invest. Several tools are available for helping you with this, they include:

- o  Real-time services for news.
  Stocks move because of news. To subscribe to services, it is important, when news that involves market changes will inform us that moves came out that could cause potential changes.

- Level 2 quotes for ECN.

ECNs, or computer-based systems, will display the available bid that is best and quotes from participants in multiple markets. Then you will need to automatically match orders and then execute them. As a subscription style service, they provide the use of real-time use of the NASDAQ book that is composed of quotes for prices from the makers market that is registered under every NASDAQ listing which can contain the OTC securities Bulletin Board.

- Candlestick intraday charts.

Candlesticks will provide some analysis that is raw and based on the auction price.

The condition that you will be positioned under should be defined and then written down. "Buy while facing an uptrend" is not enough of a specific request. "Buy when it breaks the price that goes above the trendline that is the upper part of a pattern of triangles, where the triangles preceded the uptrend which is shown on the chart for 2-minutes in the very first two hours of the day that you are trading." This has more specific verbiage and is also quite a testable statement.

Once the entry rules have been specified and set, you can scan more of the charts to ascertain the conditions that will generate the day trader's moves and which can produce a move in price for the direction that is anticipated. There is an entry point that is the potential for the said strategy. You should then decide how you will exit these trades by assessing the process.

## Deciding When to Sell

| Strategy | Description |
|---|---|
| **Scalping** | Most popular strategies.<br><br>Need to sell immediately right after the trade has been profitable.<br><br>The price target translates to "money was made on this deal." |
| **Fading** | Stocks are shorted after the upward rapid moves.<br><br>Assumptions which they are based on:<br><br>(1) Overbought,<br>(2) New buyers are ready for profits,<br>(3) Old buyers can be scared out.<br><br>Risky but rewarding.<br><br>The target price happens when buyers begin to step in. |

| | |
|---|---|
| **Daily Pivots** | Involves profiting from the volatility of a stock's daily price. |
| | Buy low for the day then sell high for the day. |
| | The target price can be simple for the reversal time. |
| **Momentum** | Trading on news releases finding trending moves that are strong and that is supported by a volume that is high. |
| | Momentum trader buys on the advice of the release of news and the trend rides until it exhibits reversal signs. |
| | The other will fade the surge of the price. Here the target price is decreased by volume when it begins. |

When faced with a decreased interest, you will need to exit the asset in the indicated stock as the volume or Level 2/ECN. The targeted profit should make way for more profit for the trades that are winning as opposed to the loss on those that trade with losing points. If your loss stop comes to $0.05 from the price entry, your target is going to be $0.05 further away.

## Patterns with Day Trading Charts

The moment that is opportune for buying stock will need to be determined by the traders utilizing specific tools:

Patterns for candlestick -this involves using the dojis and the engulfing.
The analysis that is technical- includes the triangles and trendlines.
Volume- decreasing or increasing.

There are several setups of the candlestick that a day trader can locate and find the point of entry. If used properly, the doji pattern reverses to the one that is more reliable.

Typically, you need to locate the pattern which is similar to several confirmations.

First, look for a spike in volume. This shows you of the investors are aware and accepting the price level at this point. This can be on either one or the other of the doji candle or the one following it.

Second, locate the support that is prior to this level price; the low for that day or high for that day (LOD and HOD).

Finally, locate the situation for Level 2, which covers all the orders that are open and sizes of those orders.

By following the 3-steps above, you will be able to determine whether doji's able to produce the turnaround that is on actual as well as if the conditions are favorable, takes a position.

Analysis of traditional patterns of the charts will also provide targets for the profit at the time of exits. The triangle height at the part that is widest can add to the point at which the triangle has the breakout, providing ample price for profits.

# The Limit That Is Set for Losses When Day Trading Is Important

Orders for a stop loss can be designed to limit the number of losses on a stock position that is within the security. For positions that are long, a stop loss placed under the low that is recent, or for a position that is short, the stop loss is placed over the high that is recent. Volatility can also be to blame for it. For instance, if a price for a stock moved around $0.05/minute, then the stop loss you place at $0.15 away can help with the order of entry that gives space to fluctuate with the price prior to the move in the direction that is anticipated. A clear definition will help to control the rick on the trades. When a triangle pattern is present, a loss stop is best placed at $0.02 under the most a recent low swing, especially when breakout buying, or $0.02 under the pattern.

Another strategy is to two set for a stop loss:
A physical order for a stop-loss is placed around a certain level price which will suit your tolerance

for risk. This is the amount of money you are able to lose.

A set of stop-losses that are mental during the entry criteria can be violated. So, if an unexpected turn is made by the trade, you will immediately position yourself to exit.

By deciding to exit the trades, the criteria for exit must have enough specific details to be testable as well as repeatable. You also need to set a maximum loss for each day so that you can continue to afford to fund the account and withstand the losses. There are financial and mental drains that happen when playing the stock market. If you hit a point that is draining, then take that day off. Make sure you use your plan wisely and stick to it. Plan the parameters that you will use. Remember that there is always another day that the stock market will be open, and tomorrow could be better.

After you have clearly defined the process that you will renter the trades with then you need to use a stop loss so that you will be able to assess the strategy that fits your potential needs and make sure it is within your limit of risk. If this strategy is too risky, then consider altering it to fit your level of risk better and reduce the risk factor.

If the strategy is at a level of risk that you can handle, then begin the testing procedure. Take the time to go through charts that are historical in nature so that you can find your entries, noting the target or stop loss that you placed is working or were you hit with a loss.

Pretend that you are trading following these suggestions for an about 50 stock trades to determine if this strategy is working for you. Notice if the strategy is profitable or if there are some tweaking that can be handled by you. Make sure that the strategy that you use meets all of your expectations. If it does, use the procedure to begin trading using this strategy with the demo account until you are completely confident to move on to a regular broker trading account, in real time.

If your demo account is profitable for two months or more and you have developed a strategy that works then you can proceed to utilize this strategy for day trading within a real capital market. If this developed strategy is not at all profitable, then you can begin to start over with developing a new strategy.

You should keep in mind that when trading with margin you will have a much more vulnerable account since the sharp movements price can be a bigger loss than if you were using your own money. When using margins, you are facing losing your shirt and then some since the money is borrowed from the investment firm. Margins amplify results from trading since it is not only profit but also the losses, especially if a trade fails and you crash and burn. Therefore, using some stop losses can be a crucial strategy for when you are day trading with margin.

Margin takes place when you are borrowing the money that you are investing in funding the brokerage account. Keep it in your mind though that as a day trader, the requirements to be a day trader is high, with an equity of $25,000 and this means that the margin requirements are high as well.

Day trading can be quite difficult for someone just starting out to master. It requires time to build a strategy, skill to incorporate that strategy and a discipline that is unmatched by any other career choice. Day traders need copious amounts of money and the patience and mental restraint to understand that a loss is not a negative but a learning experience.

Many of the people who have tried to day trade have failed and took with them their house and their families. Those that do not succeed, do so only because they do not have the psychological mentality to be in a high-stress environment with large sums of money hanging on their every click of a button. It requires tons of specialized equipment to make day trading profitable. There are variables that cannot be determined and a prowess to act quickly in order to become a successful day trader. The techniques, as well as the guidelines that have been described above in this entire book, can give you an example or a glimpse into what it means to be a day trader. It can help you with creating a profitable strategy. One that will bring you continued success when implemented properly and with determination and dedication.

With plenty of practice in a demo account, you should be able to develop the skills you need to take that very next step and develop a strategy and process that will grant you big gains in the stock market. Remember, once you are labeled as a day trader, it is super hard to lose that label and that is what you will be labeled the entire time you trade stock. A consistent performance that can be evaluated over time by a chart or bar graph will be able to show you what you are doing right and what you are doing wrong. It should help you to have a history of your actions and your trades so that you can adjust based on those actions or trades. You will be able to greatly improve the chance of you becoming a successful day trader by developing the mental capacity to understand the lessons you are learning and then use them to build a different plan.

# Conclusion

Thank you for making it through to the end of *Day Trading for Beginners*, I hope it was informative enough to give you the insight that is needed to make it possible for you to have the tools that you will need to achieve your goals as a day trader in the stock market.

Your next step is to sign up for an account and begin to see how much money you could be earning on any given day. If you do not have the necessary and required funds to start day trading, then I would not suggest that you do a margin since this will place you further in debt. There are several strategies in this book to help you develop one that is right for you. I have included the psychology behind day trading and what it means to fit the bill of a day trader. Over time the market can rise and fall and as a day trader you will take advantage of these market fluctuations and build a future by purchasing and then subsequently dropping the stocks that you pick up. Many people believe that day trading is fun until the stress gets to them. Make sure that you are physically and mentally fit to begin this career otherwise you may lose more than just money. Day trading takes time and money and if you do not have any of that then it is not the right job for you.

Finally, if you found this book useful in any way, a review on Amazon is always appreciated!

www.ingramcontent.com/pod-product-compliance
Lightning Source LLC
Chambersburg PA
CBHW031417210526
45464CB00005B/1932